Praise for THALASSA

"leena aboutaleb's debut is a simmering testament to grief—at once tender song, at once mouthfuls of blood. Her voice verges on prayer, repeatedly calling to her late brother, but really, it is an incantation for us, still living. 'What am I to do with all this rage?' she asks, as her poems set fire to the constraints of language. And amidst immense loss: for one's family, for one's land and people, what burns most brightly is her will to continue writing—that is, to continue on. 'Never can they love as us,' and yet, 'Never can they be martyred as us.'

Invoking a constellation of underworlds and martyrs from Gilgamesh, to Refaat Alareer, to the Legend of Zelda— she reminds us that we too, 'have a right to the Greek pantheon,' and thus, to our own narrative. Through genocide and exile, aboutaleb's poems sing with unrestrained rage, 'I link arms with my martyr, I am your witness.' These poems will haunt you long after you turn the last page, as they will mobilize you in ways poems rarely do—bend you in worship to your ancestral land, hold you in collective witness alongside beloveds in the afterlife, turn language into shrapnel, into light."

—JinJin Xu, author of *There Is Still Singing in the Afterlife*

"In *THALASSA*, leena aboutaleb makes the fantastic cerebral, the myth document, and grief into an alchemy. Everything actually is that serious, so strap in, we are going into the underworld. Dreams become portal, as is this book, but I'm wide awake and following the poet down. I don't want to miss any stone or seed in all this delicate muchness. Refrain becomes prayer, invokes the memory for the remembered to walk through. I feel their presence come forward, raising the hair on my arms. The poet looks toward their oracles until they become oracle, too. Her voice a mist making way for the horizon, and then it's the horizon. Here. Hear. Listen as this collection fearlessly rages even while it praises. *THALASSA* is a visceral and honest embodiment of grief that resists a neat bow in favor of the perpetual excavation of always the next word, line, question. This collection is fierce, gentle, not merciful, and divine.

—Jess Rizkallah, author or *the magic my body becomes*

THALASSA

poems by

leena aboutaleb

THALASSA

ISBN: 979-8-9948112-7-6

Cover art and layout by Grace Pastore

Edited by Summer Farah

Formatted by Josh Savory

www.gameoverbooks.com

Part I

Part II

Part III

For my family

"Long have we lived with the winds. We have mastered them.
Now, we join them."

—The Legend of Zelda: The Minish Cap

"And all that in his heart he wants to be,
make it be.

And all the wrong he did before, loose it.
Make him a joy to his friends,
a pain to his enemies and let there exist for us
not one single further sorrow.

May he willingly give his sister
her portion of honour, but sad pain."

— Sappho [translated Anne Carson]

Emerald-Eyed [Sacrifice of Love]

I will perish in the light for you. I will perish
the light for you. There is no thing too small
that I will not do. If I must
bring the end, I will.

I will never remove the dagger from my throat.
I will die remembering how grief ate me,
over and over, took my heart,
my eyes, my hands, the deluge of me.

For you, I will burn the world down
until the end is silvered fragments,
rivering like a scorpion's lungs.
Eternalised: the myth of a sister who lost brother.

Yousef, I will never remove the dagger.

CROSSING NO. NETHERWORLDCROSSING NO. DREAMWORLDCROSSING NO. MESOPOTAMIACROSSING NO. THEY WHO SAW THE DEEPCROSSING NO. DELUGE

Dearest Summer,

Lately I have been thinking about newness and its opponents. It is not a case of giving up on love at all. I am feeling distant from my old life. A shade passing through until I settle into the next moon-cycle. It has been a few months since this feeling began—the distance, the shedding.

Summer, I feel alone. Some hours it is the type of alone I find glorious, holy. In other moments, it is as if I am an accidental rupture in this city, rendered irrelevant, loveless in a single moment. It is so fleeting in this country, and I do not know how to find my home again. I am resting underneath the shade.

I fall back onto fluidity. I am throwing my heart in the washing machine and tossing it on the laundry-line to air. I let everything go and keep only my heart.

That is the end of the white room. I never remembered the end, but now I see it. She finds him, blood and mountains.

I'm going back to Gilgamesh. In there I will find the world-making I need. It is time to slay monsters, burrow a cave from its ribs.

Lovingly,

Part I

[*UNDERWORLD*]—GIRL, HALF-DROWNED. SOLITARY, DESPERATE, FRANTIC. SWORD IN HAND. SHE STRAIGHTENS HER BACK AND BEGINS TO WALK FORWARD.

THE UNDERWORLD is a place of crossing, of endless potential. I live, you live, we all live. The Underworld creates holding, a world where devastation and its births are rendered true. Ursula Le Guin writes, "What goes too long unchanged destroys itself. The forest is forever because it dies and dies and so lives."

It is not only a space of devastation, but of hope. In Islam, those we have buried are not actually dead; they have entered the Barzakh, where they are in a parallel existence, just as alive as you. Dreams are considered a portal and sleep a death into the unseen world.

The tide enters, mosaicing the wind. I cannot see beyond the mountains here. We are made myth; woven from light and rain. Your body is gone, and I am begging. We are made in nightfall now. Children hold our portraits up, as they recount the tale of a sister diving into the next world. Headfirst for you, Yousef.

I look for a boat, brush my hair with black seed, pinch my teeth into hard bones, elegying like a garden.

ENTRY TO THE UNDERWORLD

I am alive in another spring you are dead for. There is a mercy somewhere in this fog, in the density of this water. What do I recall of that night? The rivers of the underworld. How your ghost hums in a stilled body. The colours of blue. The shadows' probing accusations. The solace of water. You were alive, the umbrella discarded on the summer's night. The pink couches gracing Mama's hands, as translucent as water, as if Tabriyeh is more than a lake, as if your ghost sings and sings, arching a celeste symphony. You conduct water into song and so I bend my body into instrument, a sharp violin submerged in the iridescent trenches of our rivers. The Nile steals us. Bends us into eternal return. Earth holds you sweetly. Breath of graveyard always under my nails. Shapeshifters crawling from night & sun. They see you in the next life, heaven open. I dialect the flashing night, eating your disease into my skin. I barely dodged, and you are dead. Sometimes all I remember is my head colliding into the staircase, how I tasted your bones before your death to interrupt my own. There were birds once. They sing as if you are not weaving my funeral song. The dead ask of who it is I seek. I made a promise when they lowered you into soil to follow you. Yousef, I would know you anywhere.

Graveyard Visits

after and with lines from JinJin Xu's "To Red Dust (II)."

The graveyard calls every time I open my eyes. My brother, disappeared. The illness stealing you from my hands. My brother, dead in every life. All I ever wanted was to love you without bruising. I hold your life in a prayer. I am staring into your grave, crushed and unbelonging. You have forsaken me. We are on the mountain of eternity. You and our mother eating fresh figs, honeyed river suckling at us like a prophecy. I shall not see & I shall not speak. Sometimes I dream of the corridors collapsing. I am mesmerised in the graveyard. Let me return, for I am still alive. I write my name into exhale. I beg God in the fog. I beg you. Do not leave me in this sea all alone. I am still your little sister.

elegy (i); the grave

after and with lines from Diana Khoi Nguyen's "Ghost Of."

I wake in the morning, buried. Fell asleep to your corpse, body long gone. *Akh*, what have you done habeebi? Syrian wails stealing Mama's throat. How selfless a mother's love. I have spent a decade nightmaring your grave wa I will spend the rest of my life dreaming of a brother eternally twenty-five. Tell me how dates taste there, how sweet your soil, how warm the cloth. Do you feel the coffee I make us, the tea, the bateekh, what about the salt on my skin? Never meant to die that night, habeebi, I know. There is a dagger in my throat until I die for you—*if your brother dies is killed kills himself is alive you will see your brother.* I see you, habeebi, for months. The closest since we were children with shrapnel. You begin to own the shadows. You become mazes wa corridors. I wake up in a mess of tears. Is it cold underneath? Is death warm? Please, turn, look at me, face me. Tell me you are okay. I want to see our eyes one last time. Look at what you have done. Let me die with you, please, let me see our eyes once more, please, let me see your face once more. I wake in our old home. You are with our dead, laughing, cigarette lesa fil eedak wa you ask me to laugh with you, how can I ever say no? We are both dead. I wake up in your grave on my luckiest days. You died and became celestial. Time is your hands, our fates threads you witness—*I want to die* you told Baba the morning of—fortune teller inta, did jinn whisper, did you laugh? If your death was not gentle, I will kill the Angels with my hands. I swear by my heart, on my eyes. Did you smile when I put soil on your grave? I fought my way past the men for you. I refused to leave you. I held you blue for hours. I kissed your eyelashes. Please, look at me. I am begging for one more second. I want to see our eyes one more time. Please. Look at me. Tell me how I am to live and die now. How am I made to wake up in death. Tell me how can I love without craving my face open to show them what you left behind—a desperate sister—Yousef, tell me what you have done, please—I want to see you with our eyes, Yousef, *look*, you were alive once and I am dead now Yousef I am glad you are dead Yousef I will laugh with you forever Yousef I will stay in this grave with you until time ends Yousef please don't be lonely Yousef I am glad you are dead I am dead I stay alive and you are dead I eat the flowers how Mama trained us—fedayeen—I find the sea to you, Yousef, ya Yousef, habeeb albi Yousef, I am happy you are

ENTRY TO CAPITAL I
[GRIEF]

Grief bottoms like an empty-stomach soaking. I pass your birthday and stumble into your death. It is a blade severing my flesh. I am at a loss for how to find you. It is five days from your birth to your death. Should I acknowledge our family's habit of dying near their birthdays? Yousef, all week I have failed to wake. My eyes are sore between every prayer. I am under the sun, and I think of your body before your burial. Last night I was in Nablus, the crumbling city gazing into me from our window. I am beseeched by our old homes. I do not know the route from the old house. I dreamt of you walking in the corridors again, your shadow only visible in my peripheral. I cannot see you. I have lost you in the fog. In life, you tore the walls and faces open for us to hear your voice. In death, you become shy, even content. How cruel of you. I thought I saw you hiding behind my hair.

[*UNDERWORLD*]—THE GIRL ON THE EDGE OF A RIVER. LONG FROM HER JOURNEY. THE GONGS OF TIME MOVE SLEEPILY AGAINST HER ALIVE BODY. HER SWORD ON THE FLOOR.

This Horrifying Earth

after and with lines from JinJin Xu's "Against This Earth, We Knock"

language, alive
        rising to a window more than, a belonging

departure, pitiless borders
        empty the rungs of lungs, a bride

air, thins song
        hammer the teeth of pilgrims, earth calling

palms, windless plains
        formality of the maker, searching motions

veiled, picked lemons
        the spirits can-not hear you, don't cry

wind, carrying metaphor
        pluck teeth for the dead, hold respect

sheets, wrapped bodies
        mouths worn with desire, red flower

realms, morning gaze
        it is only real if the dead speak first, waiting arrival

holy, death-trails
        one foot before the other, break water

land, demanding
        its gaze raged and pitying. how foolish
        we have always been. the dead sing & sing

        & You—crawl, crawl to the scriptures & beg, beg
        till you find whose hand lays your grave

It is June, and I crave the fever of heat strokes. Kuwait, the breeze of our corniche and childhood seabed. I am digging in this earth for your body. The hope of a mint leaf. If only to have another cup with you. I am stranded in my memories, close to wishing for a death or a brush or a dream, anything as warm as the lazy recollection of our childhoods. I am looking for a night that never ends. I am looking for yesterday in tomorrow. I am in Dahab, a joint sparked in my hand, and I am naming myself. Inside the bird cage is a text, inside the text is a tunnel, inside the tunnel traces in Dibben, in Dibben the tunnels are fenced inside wire, inside the wire is abandoned medical kits and old comics, the leaflets flying in whispers of old weapons. Past Dibben and honour fictional martyrs. Pass the seabed of our childhoods and honour the pearl-divers. The first week after I learned to fly, I forgot my name.

What do death and desire have in common? I stand in the middle, the underworld aching, groaning beneath my treacherous feet. Last time I saw you alive, I sliced the watermelon, peeled mint you picked. In Portland, I landed and found you scattered. We screamed in the parking lot, open-faced, in the half-abandoned motel, how the lights began to shine in-between the night falling in on us. We strapped the mattress to the roof of the sedan and drove away from the state's crimes. In Jerusalem, your name is written in Batan al-Hawa, carried by hands who can't imagine your face. Your address as 'son of' imprinted in al-Aqsa, so each of Mama's countrymen will hold your name softly. They will hear your name in the wind, in the gardens, in the lines of our faces. Like teeth-bones, I fail to forget you. I treasure the root under pillow, as if begging. I fall into the next world. Slay all who stop me from reaching you. The children repeat the story: a sister dove headfirst into the underworld. I am in the depths, in search for a light that never falls.

The breath of a sea. The effects of such a riot. I watched you spit on a cop car on the street of our adopted city. I lost you in this alien land; our feet clumsy in new customs. You died, and I left. Akh, what have we done to Kareem, ya Yousef? Every day, I whisper to your ghost a new secret. Yousef, will you forgive me for wanting our land back? I cannot stay in this sea forever. What of soil when I've forgotten how to walk? In Amman, I learn to begin again, stumbling like a small ghazal. A heatwave lands on my skin. I burn, shading our pasts like a fallen star. Who are you and who am I? Yousef, do you remember our games? We let Kareem become King, and overthrew him each time. Do you remember the foki'a and foreigners? We tricked them into fear, moved over the guarded walls and snuck out with their treasures. Baba's Fridays? Mama's lullabies? There is a tangle in memories I refuse to forsake. I knew you. I knew you.

Last night rendered a full moon in Sagittarius. I laid in bed and meditated. I dreamed deliriously, thinking of you; the late nights in June and the devastation of appeal. I spent the day in grief, recounting and repressing. I burned myself alive, as I do every moon-fall. Somewhere love is alive, and somewhere we are there. I am bundling myself alive in Cairo's grime, ceasing the usage of machine on body, disintegrating self amongst wind. Where have you reached paradox—when did we become a paradox, trapped in a void? I am in the underbelly of my city, having chosen to be and do so. What is an Egyptian but a choice?

What bodies of water will come up then? What water will speak for me? Invoke me? Mirror me? Divine me? I am bent in worship. I know my eyes, my hips, the theory, the taste of death, daughter of seabed. Who are you, who are you?

I did not know the value of my life until he almost took it. I did not know, I do not know. Somewhere there must be an end, but lately, all I have been looking for something to end this headache. For the urge to die to disappear. I want to look under the table and find myself again. Why have you hidden my corpse? Inevitability is the next. The ghosts sing, and you pretend not to hear.

I feel filthy all the time in America. Emptied beyond my own understanding with a desperation rivalling a headless chicken. I never wanted it. I never wanted to leave our seabed and grow paradox. Expertise in running on air, letting the wind push my soles onwards. Lucky when feet touch the ground; when safety is real and not a figment of imagination. We are living off someone else's credit card. They write us, our bodies and lives, as tax exemptions. See: orange trees lined by the hundreds willowing in my eyelids. Mama says ibn Sirin translates it as wealth. Maybe my rizq was lucky; maybe I am lucky to survive on nothing but air. Take air and turn it into earth. I see him. Light seeping in, sneaking past him. Trace our footsteps. Do you think we will last forever? Who will I become when I die?

I know the old tongues, our eyes, the odes of the winds. The shape of it all—how devastation is patient, a strawberry ripening on the edge of a mouth. My eyes, the sign; stolen heartbeats, forage anew; our childhood will end the world.

Let me tell you about my brothers. Let me tell you about my dead brother. Let me tell you who he is: how he lost his face until God called mercy. Let me tell you of the forever, the piece of me still in his grave.

Yousef, I will drain the sea. I will reach its end, chained to Azazeel's home, weeping, a call for mercy.

Memory, Isle of Blest

after and with lines from JinJin Xu's "There Is Still Singing in The Afterlife."

We carry the dead,
the winds change, the pilgrims prostrating

bellied truths & I forgot my way home in the heat.

I am singing
in the shower, love in flesh, watermelon cooling

the sheets concealing your absence, my absence,
how I ran when waking to the ancient terrors

our fates, star-clustered your face, grasping the eldritch of me.

remember the language between us &
no thing left to say.

my mouth chalk full of blisters & I fulfil my inheritance

remember hundreds of years
before the sea before we gave Greece
its fortune and myths.

remember my name in the next life

the river of forgetfulness &
the river of oaths and hatred
beneath her, next to her, a pit.

misspeak my name, still entangled
in shared worlds somewhere

you will find me, *eventually,* this I know,
this I declare an eternal truth.

come—we loved once,
I can no longer recall how but once, once
we loved.

In the beginning was (*light, absence, slated*)

—a long night.

you become a ghost drenched
in the afterlife. your tongue,
a sea of souls who once
spoke like you.

I tried to tell them, I am of the night.

Arabic: an everywhere in [of], silver, effacing the land, the seas,

If there is one thing that can be written with joy, it is the eulogy for all that has been and will never be again. Under God, the beginning of a universe. Return with me.

Daphne, the Oracle

I find over the course of my small life that those we love will leave us. Eternal glory to love! The ecstasy of our childhood will cloud over our break, soothing its edges into the monster we love. 'Monster' as a creature of hurt, not born of evil. A yeti builds a home, a ghoul pounds salt, a warlock hangs their laundry. The real monster has always greed. The Calamity, the last Scourge. I covet the wind.

I love the temporary. I have to go. This portal is closing, and I am another person. I only know the night sky, and how when I stare at the moon, I remember you. Where does everything go? Into non-being, which is to say, everything. The flame or phoenix? A circle has no beginning nor end; it pulls taunt on a repetitive thrum, the fruits of my land handed to me by the men of my land. I know my country. I am a fragment splintered along the riverbed of my ancestors' and their lovers.

There is a dialectical relationship between hope and despair...the state of misery. I find my ghosts lurking in the shadows, sitting on Persephone's tongue picking bits of seeds. I am a speck of violence, an eternity of love. A ship is rotting at the bottom of my sea, so I work to remake the kitchen, the windows, the garden. My dead guiding me past old loves and exhausted cities.

Persephone, I understand. May I rest here, only a small while longer?

I have eaten the pomegranate. One seed from heaven. One seed for you.

PART II

ENTRYWAY TO CAPITAL II
[PERSEPHONE'S CHAMBERS]

I am too comfortable being alone, too greedy when hands appear, too selfish when the world breaks. Full blue skies and stars spinning. Glory and gore. What have I got to prove?

Ego-death: remove attachment from desire. It is easier to do when you are being desired. It is easier to do when everything is in place, waiting for you to take your seat at the dinner table. The party goes on without you and doesn't that hurt?

Amman, a plateau. What is to be gained from this landscape? A stagnant emptiness. I don't know where the idea of rest fled me, but yesterday it rained all day and I grieved. I flooded in the rain. I am waiting for a magic to be released, open the water and not drink salt. The world spins and spins and people are alive, people are dying, and I am here. I am here.

I saw my face, distorted into eldritch. I clawed it off and burned it. I am glad I am not eighteen anymore. I am glad I am where I am.

CROSSING: THE LOVER AS THE ONE I DISAPPEARED FROM, THE DISAPPEARANCE ETCHED IN LOVE, LOOK LOOK LOOK!!!!!!

DO YOU THINK I DON'T LOVE? I AM OF FIRE OF AIR I AM CLAY AND SOUL. I WILL NEVER LOVE ANYONE THE WAY I LOVE YOU—LOVE[D];LOVE. GILGAMESH ME. PICNIC ON ARAFAT AND CARAMEL. LET ME SHOW YOU THE EYES! STOP!

THE PROPER DUTY OF MAN IS TO ACCEPT MORTAL LIFE, TO STATIC PATIENCE, TO WAIT FOR THE CAVE AND RECEIVE PROPHETIC WORD, TO TAKE THE HOLY TEXTS AND DIVINE FROM MIASMA & OLD SPEAK [AS IN I WILL TEAR THE WORLD DOWN, OPEN, APART IF ONLY FOR YOU].

ENTRYWAY TO CAPITAL III
[DESIRE]

after Sappho

All night long the song of violets between myself and the bride. Call the men, for no more than the bird with a piercing voice shall we sleep in a true rest. I want to suffer in myself, this much I know. Mother, Persephone, Daughter of Ghost. Gilded arms and doom. What monster awaits the way under the Mountain? I am waiting in sacrifices, the shades of light—*poikilos*. The forest overhead, the gaze of the All Seeing and Unseemingly. There is a myth of light in this world, the Undertaking of a sum. The causation of a self gone astray in the field of banshees and kelpies. Flesh flees in pursuit. Sing to us. Lead me down the dewy riverbanks, all night long. Let the nightingale flee from the perch. Put my heart in my chest, the wings taking flight when I look at you for even a moment—*shh*, no speaking. No Tongue breaking and thinning, my fire stuttering in your gaze. Fortune teller. I am and dead. If only I could win. Stars around the moon, hiding their luminous forms, whenever full she shines the Prophet's splintering, face fresh and silvered on the earth. I seek and long after my dripping, past the time of my death. The blaming winds and well-wishing terrors carry you off. For you, of white goat and gauzed ghost, I pour the wine over the streets as an ode to ancestors. For you, for us. Eternal. The day is near. My mother veils me. I, the bride. The Herald came, and in it, the rest of Asia in an imperishable fame and famine. The glancing girl from the Holy lands, likened to idols of myth, is holy all together. Sing the holy song. Sing a holy song. Straight up the air goes, right back to God. Untamed on solitary mountains, held separate on the island as I call your name. As you take me in. There is a share, as long as you want it.

Mythos

after Sappho

I shall love weapons. Note our beautiful times and beautiful land. Tie together a gentle crown of anise. Let the woven violets lose and regain their petals. Let the garlands rest on the softness of my throat. Let the motion of light frame my portrait. Let me lose myself in my longing. I am on the world again, seeped in Holy, my Land making. Sweet almond oil, fresh tides of jasmines, rosemary water, crushed hibiscus. The dazzle of dawn, my father gathers a lamb. The bride is made of miracles and sacrifices, as aching and hidden as time's cycle. I am no one's beloved. My light stretches the sea, rinsing its salt from banks. You, all teeth and beautiful cheekbones, my drowsy reflection, the morning ache and nightly ritual. A fawn trembling in grief. Let the moon hang herself for you. Our memories exiled, leaking away. I am broken in longing. A grievous wish. You stole me the first night I slept in the new land, so close to the pilgrimage. Bridegroom, the veil of purity against the evening light. The moon cries, wishful Andromeda hidden behind a laurel tree and sweet flowering cloves. You pick an apple, unknown to us besides nativity. The mountains are your shepard. Unable to reach. Blest, blessed, my beautiful groom. My form stepping from the fog. In the night, Astarte returns to renew me into your wish, your sapling, your mythweaver.

I love you. Kan ya makan, a princess let her hair fall down the tower, letting the daring climb upwards, find the clouds and touch the stars. Where does the world end and begin? It's two years and I avoid my grief, harbouring it like a secret port; a tunnel into self. I come in seasons and only at your hand and will. There must be a spell to change the current, a card to spin a future into almond blossoms. I miss you when I see you. Do you ever wait for a chorus of angels to drop down? Mourning doves the future into now; the present constantly moves between gone and untold. When the world erupts and the sea comes to eat, letting earth claim its right, where will you be? Write me back. I'm on the edge waiting for a call that will never come. All I dream of is jumping. I'm starving myself again, watching the hollows of my cheekbones reappear. I am punishing myself for a last moment, a last call, a last wish. I am not brave enough to meet your eyes even as the sword hangs from torso. There is a self, a shadow or ghost of us haunting the underworld, living a dream burnt from rotten fruits, the blushing of pomegranates. I hold a crown on my head, waiting for fate to open the door and eat me alive. I long for the days where my bones are picked, to walk along the desert until I arrive at the sea. There is an end and beginning. I'm looking for love in ruins, how dilapidated the city has fallen, and still we stand.

Once I mourned you. Nourished and fed you. Love on a dinged silver spoon, better than we could dream to afford. The lights are bruising over here. Back then, in the old car and burnt eyes, we swam relentlessly. It kept raining and we kept going, as determined as our mothers. The first day, I thought of a joke and you embodied it. We blew it on a long night and series of holidays, laughing at the lavishness. Versailles defanged and dethroned. O, oh, if only we knew the rich: how wealth is a sleeper, creeping slowly around backbones. We assured ourselves nothing could change, the water still dripping from our clothes and the lights still bruising. We ate sugar with our porridge and bought flowers instead of stealing them. I never thought I would miss the lights or the punishing sea. We laughed, sure of ourselves in the way only children can be. I wish I had known that even a disgraced king is still a king. Monarchy is always kissing split blood. Can you tell me who we have become? A split so severe I sometimes see you in doubles. How do you hold yourself? How do I hold you? How do you hold me? I see you and feel a missing, an abstraction. The old flat closed, the roads emptied. I set the table and you do not arrive. We are all here, still, in the midst of the world; its capital marking our lives in brutal strokes. And you, so far away, locking a gilded door. Can you see us still?

Instead of suffering for man, she suffered for God. First: Hawa. The origin. Her name, a meaning unto itself. Back-biter, heaven-flesh, man's ribs, snake-whisperer. I call for Maryam in my debt. Oblivion, husks of palm trees, vowed silence. I want to talk to you about womanhood as it pertains to me, but I find myself in a bowed silence. I sit under Maryam's tree and find a piece of myself left after my birth. The shadows calling the letters until my name is made soft and tender from my palm tree. I received a charm of a golden palm tree, immortalising myself and fate. Each time I fall in love, I bear fruit. Such generosity is only necessary in the desert, when the true world is hungry, sleepy, feeding, drowsy, roaring. I love waking up because it means the palm reading of my childhood friends lives true. My body remade by desire. Tell me what I look like in the light. The pomegranates are rotting in my stomach and still, I want to know their secrets. The phone line screeches and Issa intones God's will onto my mortal body. I forget: I am all clay, all dirt, all blood. Just a human girl staring at the moon for a second chance. I have been living in the underworld for the last three years; grief so thick and lonely it became a new rib, a new womb. It ate my eyes out and I left my shoulder in my brother's grave. I was 23 and tender. Still so small. All I did was choke for years, called the mountains to protect me, and begged God.

[*UNDERWORLD*]—THE GIRL, HER SWORD REFORGED, PERSEPHONE SETTING FRUITS ON THE TABLE, HER GARDEN SPRINGING FORTH.

ENTRYWAY TO CAPITAL IV
[PRIESTESS]

Let him be happy. Let his grave be easy. Let him rest. Let him be loved. Please tell him I miss him. Please tell him I love him. Please tell him an eternity with him is not enough. Protect my brother. Let my brother be happy, o God, let him be happy in his new life.

I spent the last few mornings bent in a special kind of worship. The last ten days sunder an echo into the divine. The ground came up, erupting at my feet and I knew my brother was laying his hands on my shoulders as he gathered my prayers like coins in the hereafter. God is my witness. I know what I pray for, but I do not know when the angels will come to avenge my name. A shade of another world's midnight edges pulls its hand out towards me, taking off my bridal veil. A nightmare brewed, a hero is made. Let us ask for forgiveness, for the earth is a wealth.

Causation and Collapsation

I still cannot bear to face the mirror. The ghost of your face hanging in mine like an undead image. A sister missing, a brother long gone, a brother hidden. I grieve and look for the honeysuckle. As if you will be found alive in the fog. Let time strike true; the ringing gong in glory of eternal love. Look at me, how I am wrought and astray. I am stranded, lost in the grasp of eternity.

ENTRYWAY TO CAPITAL V
[MARTYRS]

My brother, etched into history like the myths. I keep my family alive eternally, so everyone who looks into my face will see whose love carries me through the sea time and again.

Ramadan

I awake a new-born fawn. I shake the soil and the forest off my coat. I love my mother. I love my father. I love my brothers. I pull at the ground. I become land. I become memory. I am made memory. I am made in memory. The forest hears me, the leaves marking an eternity I exist. I make my brother a victor. I make history obsolete. I turn you into a night, never-ending. We sink at the river. Let it soak. The river kisses my eyelashes, as I kissed yours. The sun comes to eat, settling its knives and lovers to brush my hair. Look at me, how I wander and become stillness. Am I still there? Am I still here? Persephone, our light shared between our worlds. You are the only one who knows where my body is hidden, buried. Tell me where I am, of who I become now. I am learning, once more, the water. Wait for me. I am still alive. Let me speak through the gaps of the wind and its waking. I love you. I love you.

ENTRYWAY TO CAPITAL VI
[GRIEF]

The world rifts in an endless tide, one lick of eternity unravelling its grief. I tell Summer I want to unplug myself from the electricity cable and sever the algorithm's false heartbeat from skin. The ozone coos and I curl myself, hitching a ride on the stars to make it to the moon. Eternity is dying and I am splintering easily, negligibly on the surface. I push out soil and close my eyes, and for once there is true silence. I do not have bills to pay on the moon, no expectations of love, no dreams or hopes. I am a shadow of a girl collapsed and eternal, dying and dead, alive and mourning. Salivate at the knowledge that no temporality rings true, no time linear, no permanency exists. I pay my dues and debts to the fleeting temporary of myself. I know which seasons bring me, cradling me into a girl callously undone or scorchingly alive. I eat fire and throw myself off a cliff without a second glance. The moon rung full two days prior. A ruthless knife, burying its blade underneath a tidal of tears. O, how she rings. O, how she rings.

A series of mangled bodies; I open the rip-tide of medical malpractice. Seven years and no one wants to say what feasts upon my brother's skin. The waiting room: my eyes do not *tap tap tap* incessantly like a batch of fresh narcissa severed from flesh. A flower sunk and sinking in the river nymph. I am remade into a river spirit, a ghost of the waters we once called home. I forsake my flesh for the tiding blisters. I fall asleep at the cafe, four shots of espresso in. I pull apart the stone tiles of the bakery with my hands, counting each line and indent for a shape of reality. Time has fled me, become one with my flesh. We are melded together into a new myth. Eternal and nothing. Time is a passage and everything, everywhere, all at once. It flushes and I cry. Sage is crushed fresh, burning in tea. My great-aunt used to hide the smell of her cigarettes with every bundle of land. The majnoona leaves cover the wind, crossing more distances than the bodies watering it. A pulsating beat of the earth, and in it there is no end; no respite. Let time fall. Let my body end. Leave us weeping. I want nothing more than to drown.

Wind Waker

after Summer Farah

There is always a prophecy: it is born
blood-soaked on you or
you, born bloodied, soaked in the drenches of prophecy.
Brutalist, the age of awe, of living, of firsts, of firsts—
at 17 I wanted to be divine, a subject to be admired
as Helen, as Penelope, a torrent of cruelty, of blades & curses
my blood, its windchimes and rushing rivelets,
a lung split open inside ribs
& what do we deserve? It is past midnight, almost fajr,
when you die and the prophecy keeps me awake that very night.
I am no more delirious than usual, no more silent than always,
my beauty a blade I sharpen in my silence, my silence a collapsing
bridge, the monsters
under the blood moon always calling their bodies back from Tarturus &
sometimes I am lonely
a girl, still somewhat seventeen, twenty-eight, and still I wonder
how to plan my wedding
will they ask if I leave a seat for you still?
How did your brother die?
How will yours die? Yousef, I look for you in this flood, this deluge,
this silly life of mine, of yours, of your face settled in my face,
and my collarbone buried in your grave
& all year, I wait for June and July,
I am patient for devastation—to peel my skin *back* and remember
You were alive once. I have tried to outrun my own fate.
I slipped my skin & joined the lament
a tree, a forest, a bird, the sunlight—
What happened?
I awoke, and you know the rest.

Graveyard Visits: Confessional

Every time I return to your ending, I find myself at the beginning of time. My brother, eternal. It was October. I came to say goodbye. I sat with you, and the mother deer and her bambi stood on your grave's edge, blessing you and staring into me. *The pitiful girl and her dead brother.* Your grave is filled with ladybugs crawling on the grass and so I forsake my fear of land's creatures as I kneel in prayer for your soul. Each time I return to you, I find my legs metalled, each step heavier than the last. It is difficult to come with anyone to see you. As if the spectacle of my grief is too humiliating to be witnessed by even our mother. If I could decree memory, then I would surely never leave your grave again. Let me carry you, as you carry me. What kind of sister would I be otherwise? I hope you rejoice when you hear my steps. I hope you know there is nothing in this world I want more than our family.

With all my love, from the echoing thrum of my heart,
Your beloved little sister.

الثكل

A woman cleans the gravesites. *I can't bear to see trash around my husband.* Her husband is dead, like you. Today I did not bring you flowers. I brought myself, dressed against the code. I knelt and tried not to cry, so as not to hurt you. I bury myself with you a little more every time, Yousef. A silly devotion.

I do not know how to conjure you back, Yousef.

PART III

[*UNDERWORLD*]—THE GIRL. HER SWORD. AN ARMY OF GHOSTS.

Bridegroom

A percussion alluding to light. The exaltation
of our eternities, of the very first beginning,
dancing in our zaffe. We bent time into an unending.
We begin and begin and begin anew, a fostered
love where we yearn to be stripped past rubble
into beings, human and simple,
in the coming of a cool spring. The gongs are ringing,
calling glory to the ripe persimmons as red
and decadent as our sun-kisses.

And so the light flashes, filling prayer under God's dedication
from the honey bee and ants to us, young and torrented,
still too selfish to be true to one another.

Like my foremothers, I am spent under my namesake
the date trees lining and dotting our landscape.
My love, how dashing is the face of your arrogance
in the window of our union. How tragic
your gooseflesh rings in the beginnings of our children.

Our worlds, once singular and ringing, coming together,
merging the light and its night.

There's a parade for us. Confetti streaming and fresh meringues. In every scene, I picture you. Let miracles run wild. Watch for my gaze. Time is a refusal of waiting. I have one foot crossed over the other, each in another timestream. Kairos. Khronos. Red tea too-sweet. The heat of our countries blazing. It's miraculous how we ache. Grieve for us. On the precipice of a cinematic revelation my phone rings, shattering the wind and I scrape my knees, learning a new trick to being a protagonist. The only way I'm made real is in this script. The director gives me shape to inhabit. Ghosts are coming and going. I watch their migration routes, hungry. Eternity and her prospects are such a wind-up. All teasing and no jokes. Living only matters when I know I'm going to die soon enough. Can you tell me where I am meant to be? A river curls up my shoulders and I drown in its bank. It's stunning. Look at how much I love you. Look at my invincibility on our sets. In these carefully painted worlds of ours. It's so beautiful.

The moon is calling full, its emergence singing. All I ever wanted was you. A home, fresh bread, a sweet love. Hold me tender. I tore myself apart, left my bones for suckling. The marrow a sweet birth, decadent rosemary and pulled wildflowers on the table. You magic a reality with each demand. Look at me, a sacrifice learned from ancestry. Maryam's yolking, my shades. The air silvering, littered with mercury, all in the break of love. I am but nothing. I am but everything. I learn anew in the light's washing. Blushing sweetly, an apple of heaven. Can you see the sun? Languishing in the other world, how gorgeous the rotting fruits sing for us. I am waiting under God's mercy. A being of clay and creation, my free will a sea. I love you. Come, come. Eat my teeth. Let my body rot, let my body love, let my body air. The birds are singing. The birds are singing, and I cannot tell you if I am dead or alive.

In which the sea cries

I have created a thousand and seven daydreams dedicated like a martyr. A ritual, wherein light and its fog are borne witnesses to testament. In a thousand and seven lives, I have loved you. Every night I pick apart a different way to fall in love with you. Every morning I wash you off myself, and I am so good at it. I lie and lay. I know the matter of which we are splintering. I know the collapse of your teeth, how your smile no longer begets our memory. Time is a river, a lake, a sea. She cries and cries, bemoaning our endings. How many times have we continued like this? Listless, as if we had not only a few moments ago been in a love so unending that even karma paid its debts at our feet. You do not lie awake dreaming of me, and I spend my days forgetting you effortlessly. The sea cries and cries as delirious as we once were. She washes our grave-stones as the moss lives on the monument of us. Our country fractures, and I know it is not from the weapons. Your eyes are missing, and I am waking. Let us prove the fates and her sisters wrong. Let love ring its eternal glory. Dress me in the grove of our garden. Put the stones back in the walls. Find me again.

Scorpio Eclipse: Portal

Dearest Jessi,

There is a world that will not hurt like this—a better world, close enough to touch. I must give up my world to enter unburdened, my ego bloody and killed on the threshold. There is only so much wishing one can do, only so far love can go. There is a divinity I have forgotten. I made myself mundane. My divinity will protect me, keep me alive. I only have to give it the chance. The bakhour has burnt away. What do I do with all of this hurt? In the fire I felt clean, anew. I have let my fear alter me for so long. Here. Hear. Let my soul be my light. Guide me into the world that is waiting for me.

Frightfully Yours,

ENTRYWAY TO CAPITAL VI
[SPECTRAL LINES]

Ruptured Interiors

Did you ever return? Did you choke on fire? Am I a foolish, silly little girl with all of this imitation and hope? I am trying to live up to the giant of your love. I want to say I am from you, from my mother, linked in a sacred triforce to my brothers. Our blood builds a family. I am scared, Jiddo, that sometimes I am too shadow, all fire, wisps of wind. The world is asleep. Fog thick. I want to describe for you the sky today. Hang gilders. Liberation. It will not last. But today it is so beautiful, and so today I remember you. 17 and a country stolen. Did you grieve? Loss, so loud in the silence of what is not said. The Hebrew news, as if we speak bastard. Were you loyal out of duty or love? I know you as flight. The grandfather I made impossibilities for. My Jiddo who kept me a secret every morning as fajr called, wrapping us in a world only you remember now. I wonder about you, mostly mundane. What cigarettes did you smoke? Did the cancer scare you? How fiercely did you love my mother, your daughter? What flowers made you homesick? The olive tree you hid in your sock on the plane to America. How would you look at me today? I still hear you calling me. *Wein Leena, wein Leena hilweh, wein habibity Leena?* I am across the world, Jiddo, and so lonely. Stars in my hair, stars in my eyes, abyss and void. How did you find the courage to live? How did you find the courage to die?

Hijacked Interiors

Jiddo, I have lost count of the days. I have become haunted. Hunted. You refused the nationality and I refused the country. What if it's someone I love next? I think of the pink living room; the ghosts who watch. I never thought before of those who made me until judgement sought its claim into me. It was a party, and I woke up crying for my brother. *Laugh with me, I know you're running late.* The Palestinian sitting in his words more than ever before. I dream of my dead in Arabic. I dream of my dead in Arabic, the echoing lilts of their voices. A man in my flat laughs at my accent. I am made spoiled, princess, bourgeois. All Nablus. Waiting for my lost crown. We both know he'll still kiss me in between the static. I go to your grave and find nothing. I go to my brother's grave and find a well. I go to the land and find relief. I go to country and find self. Jiddo, it has been so long since I slept in the centre of violence. Jiddo, do you remember the years I begged to go back? The years when I didn't? What is identity but a card? At a panel, they are fraught with third-worlds and I am simmering, a freshly slaughtered lamb, the rage roasting me tender. *Arab with a passport.* I turned my back to empire at fifteen. I fled at nineteen. Amman laughs, *what do you mean you can't talk to foreigners?* All I taste is blood in my mouth constantly. I will die and still taste a drop of metallic; the hatred turned shrapnel. Jiddo, I have never not known myself and yet I want to tell you I keep reading Basel all over again. Six months. Two hours. *I have my found my answers.* Despair is manufactured. My body still hanging on the baptism, dreaming of tearing the eye of the river open again. I demand a witness. I do not care about foreigners, their eyes, their mouths. Let war wash on their statehood; eradicate the button. They can never be as brave as you. Jiddo, I love you. Jiddo, I understand now. Jiddo, what am I to do with all this rage?

Spectral Memory

Your grandfather purposely failed the year three times, so he could help his brother. The brother who shakes your hand and condemns you in the first breath. You smile and thank him. Your grandfather had a whip of jokes, but the whip was for your mother and the jokes were for the rest. Your grandfather was a nuclear physicist, but have you been to the region? Your grandfather was a Gemini, your grandmother a Libra. There's a joke somewhere there. The last memory I have of my grandfather is him trying to make me smile as he was dying. The french toast to make me happy. Extra whip cream. I cannot remember the jokes he made. I only remember fear, for the first time in my life. I looked at my grandfather and his skin scared me. His cancer scared me. I wanted nothing more than to have my Jiddo back. That version of Jiddo was not him. This version of Jiddo was him. I still feel the gulf of his love. Grandma gave me all his documents. She confides: I, his favourite. So she passes me his heirlooms. His old lighter. His passports. His first address in Chicago. An album of him growing old in Jordan. She pins me a gilded rose and a gold bracelet. I am honoured in death. What did you say in the dark, Jiddo? When you rose so early in the dawn's light, as I climbed my way up to you every morning. What did we do? What did we laugh about? Did you ever think 'Amti Hind would become my favourite? Did you think I would return to the not-country? Did you ever look at me and think *the legacy of my blood lives in this girl and she's all curly hair*? How much of you is in me? Did you look at my father and think of the compliments and contours he would give me? Did I become lesser somehow, in the dialect of Arabs, that my father is neighbour and not brother? You spent Saturday mornings at the fish market with my father, and he carried on taking us even after you died. I begged for years to see your grave. They said you are buried next to a girl who was the same age I was. I like to think we are both keeping you company. I have seen you in my dreams, in flashes. At my wedding; during my move; in the old living room. I carry you and wonder what you would say to me now, what you have been saying to me for years.

ENTRYWAY TO CAPITAL VII
[DUST]

October

I look for your gaze in the horrors of tomorrow. I dream you become a feda'i, scarf around my hips. I have slumbered in the belly of the beast too long. Rejected presence and took flight. *There is nothing they cannot do.* They can never wake up as us. Never can they love as us. Never can they be martyred as us. It is October, and suddenly my mother is full of words about prison. It is October, and suddenly I cannot look. It is October, and I am hidden in the night, wheat paste running down my forearms as if blood. As if justice. As if. I do not know what difference is made; split; incurred. The presence of remembrance. Whose eyes do you seek? Translation as underworld, underbody. What are the artefacts of dispossession? What is atonement? Empire outsourced. Let me kiss the fear. What comes first? Allah, watan, el malek. I am begging for a witness. When has language been such a burden? When has sight been such a loss? Every night, I am embroiled in turmoil. I am at sword's length from the enemy: I am screaming in the middle of a building; I am tearing way out of the abyss; I am pulling my fist, my foot, my boot back. Violence becomes me. I burn a passport. I hold secrets. I remember the movement of God. *Are you scared?* All I hear is the drones in the walls. Are you? Can you hear me still? I watch a city burn. *Don't be so scared of the fire.* Its warmth, the desire raging it and becoming ravaged. It is God's will. Who do you bow for? My aunt weaves tales of Jerusalem, Nablus, Jericho. Cities crumbled, cities hungry, cities starving. *Tell me about the country.* There are no words left to say. What has been said is said. I emerge from the egg, a snake, mouth wide open for the kill—

Languaging Memory

You, we, I. Do you remember? He was your age now. Tall. The rifle. Four, then seven, then ten. Qalandia. Ramallah. September. Yarmouk. Kuwait. Can you say the name? Everyone wants futility. Let them languish and despair, disguising pride in cowardice. I am born in fugitive, the cover of eternity clothing me. If not this life, the next. If not us, the next. *They will forget.* I list massacres in my head by the decade. What has been stolen cannot be said. What do I know of theft? What do I know of loss? My lungs permanently damaged from the teargas. I am scared for my womb. April, the fear of motherhood. What was I supposed to tell him? Maryam called. Did they think one begets emptiness? Father of what? The strikes left on me like an infant suckling. My daughter will hold them as I have. Like her mother, she will grow into her mother. The banner of fire setting her aflame. The prison, the sound bombs, the stampedes. I grew with hands tracing the walls in search of radios, training paranoia. My mother's daughter. Her eyes and her will. I know the shape war leaves. I, too, played between the abandoned homes. Stuck my fingers through the bullet holes like a portal, a looking glass into the other side, imagining the width of despair as if I am not made of my mother's fractured hips and begotten memory. I still know the shape of the bunker. We spent twenty years not eating lentils afterwards. *Would you give birth in Palestine?* I can no longer wait. I remember forever now, embraced in the still death. How memory becomes tangible, genetics permanently altered. *I speak like my father.* How beautiful you are, habeebi. To'burni. I'll see you on the other side, our child naming the fruits.

The universe began on October 7. I am in the middle of a haunting, having slept through the passage of the long middle. There is ground shaking under my feet, and I remember the grasp of my mother's hands on my hips when I first learned to move. I am lucky by the 3s and 7s, asunder in the seabed constantly. In therapy, we work on a hypnotic exercise. *What do you see?* The sea. I am on a makeshift raft in the middle of a storm. This image becomes me for years. I know the sea as my opening; the beginning and end of time. One day, we will all drown. Right now, we are still in the earth. What pledge do you have for me? Who should I swear fealty to? What kingdom should I bow my head for? What man should I take on my knees? I walk through endless tunnels only to end up nowhere and everywhere. *If you come back to Amman, I'll drag you by your hair.* O, God, I know how thick the mist and how desperate the gaze. *Where are you happy?* In another world. I am burning the house down in therapy a few months later, the altar fresh of rage. Let the angels come to reap. I no longer want your hands. Your offering is cheap. We no longer come to eat. I have watched them wash the riverbank of its eyes. What use of words do I have underneath empire's muzzle? What movement of resistance is not a declaration of glory? I abandoned you once. I love you still. The world is swept, and I am a witness.

Inheritance

I break a mirror of three. My cats break even more. *Evil eye*, I hear my father's voice echo in the back of my head. When my mother's wedding china smashes on the hard floor, she murmurs a prayer. Mirror images. I see you see you see me through sea, blue, and Etel's yellow mountain. I see her mountain in Berlin and cry. Arab apocalypse. I want to unravel my ghosts. I want to press their laundry and brew sweet tea. I want them comfortable in my skin, crossing the realms. How many thousands of years did it take so we could exist? A bomb silences the aeons foretold. I am only an echo of my mother, filled with the brightness of her love. I exist because of my mother. I carry my mother's land for her. Indomitable. Reflections are mirrored in reflections; we are water, Summer. So Etel says. 53 days, and all I think about is how we become our mothers. Reality cannot deal with itself, and so enters the urgency of the poet: the keepers. Etel says this, Summer. I am frightened. Let my labours move a stream if not a sea. I have pulled the bells of revenge and became water. 57, all I have in my spine is an unwavering gaze. I am my mother's daughter. Bint immi. *Bint mama.* In Berlin, the taxi driver spits out his coffee upon the understanding of truth; the dialect of body in nationality. *But your Palestinian is perfect.* Yama. I cry in Berlin, in Cairo, in Amman, in Salwa, in the end of time when I am called to witness my life I am called as my mother's daughter I am called as my mother I become *Leena bint Tesreen.* It is my mother who walks me, guides me; it is my mother I see in the expo marker and the kites; the sea and its love; the garden and the land. I did not know peasantry, but I wrapped *Yama* like wool around my body as if it will keep me safe in this violence. *Mirror, mirror, will you tell me when they will fall?* Sword and neck. Expo marker and kite. Illusions and mere dust. Fires and mountains. A land hostage on my throat, doused in gold. My mother picking stones from the river and sea.

What about witnessing do you want to remember?

None of it. I want to remember no scream, no agony, no grief, no rage. I want to remember the warmth of victory. The underside of a belly filled with hot food. A cat, a donkey, a dog, a bird asleep safe. A child in school. A poet with only a marker. A newspaper filled with journalists. A sea blushing in love. A crossing arbitrary with no fees. Passports as souvenirs from a mythical time. A natural death in soft sleep between the night. A contact rinsed, glasses fixed, braces tightened, back-pain mitigated, dialysis functioning, cancer centres open. Periods as a right, birth care accessible. Going to the doctor is a breeze. What conditions? What trauma? What prognosis? What is in the body of a whale, Yunus-whole? Books. Keys. Maps. Villages. Soap factories. Libraries. Worship. What is next? The oil jumping in the baker's oven. God's hands at the end. If only betrayers and greed, infilators and capitalism, an enemy would be as simple as a plain. Why is there a list? How many genocides can a month hold? How much does violence take? Double blooded. I pray for my parents to keep their minds. I pray my body has no need for heroes. Did you misunderstand me? The break in the gaps. I wish for dawn to break. Let me only write about mundane and love. I link arms with my martyr, I am your witness. I am paralleled lives; at once I hold a gun, pull the trigger; at once, blood pools from my mouth and I know God; at once, I am in a tunnel, my hips sinking onto you; at once, I am bride, veil coated in dust; at once, I am villain, subhuman, fighter. At once, I am woman in rage; teeth marked with knives. I trace the river back and forth until traversing. Of small deaths within life. Endless crossing. My heart, entirely dependent on yours. What are we if not a nation?

Jiddo, today I write to you on another death day. Today I mourn a giant of a man, Refaat Alareer and his loved ones. I mourn for his children, his wife, and for the entirety of Palestinians. I am sat in Berlin, a month prolonged in Europe, rotten food on the edge of my lips and I still say bismillah despite. It is not God I have a grievance with; it is humanity. I scorn Arabs and wage bored wrath against foreigners. *The food is bland, the coffee is bad.* Every action comes a turning point of enshrining us. *I miss garlic*, Julia laments. We are in this body, split across Asia. We count the solidarity stickers and rip the posters, archiving a digital count of which city is allowed to witness our return. The za'atar in Berlin makes my tongue ache, flavour translated all wrong. The sumac smells like oil and not berry. Coffee is burnt and the milk is off. The wind is a knife and everything upsets me. I am born distanced and all at once. Mama stared at the feda'ai, her gaze flooding his. This, the only truth to withstand time. The rifle, I know, the same on Seedo's. I know, the burst of blood. I know, the interrogation rooms. I know, not even prisoner but disappeared. A silence rings between the blasts. Is this cowardly of me? I count the minutes meticulously at the border despite having avoided interrogation for the last year. I crossed the threshold in Berlin, Jiddo, and for the first time my hands were not swiped for explosives. The guard ushers me, *minnah wa finnah* and what I have is no replacement for a rifle. Poetry: man-made eternity in the face of liberation. A beautiful look into God before death. I know at once the heat of the sun, how Kuwait burnt us all. Jiddo, Farah tells me *orange trees* and I am indebted to a dead language lost in the thrush of reclamation. I write a thesis and declare ghosts, the symbols bastardised in the tongue of sulta. A man asks me to explain and I said, *what would you do if you read a poem about olive trees?* Thousand years and dead. What should I say now? Jiddo, I wear your kuffiyeh around my throat still, the last decade soaking it in the teargas of empire, begging to be born a new tomorrow, the rinds of watermelon leaking on the street with no concern for starvation.

ENTRYWAY TO CAPITAL VIII
[SPECTRAL LINES]

28 June, 2024

It has been four years since. 29. 25. Barely on the threshold of all that rot, of all that is holy. I cross plains to reach you. Your spine is inconceivable, as far-reaching as our seabeds, the eternity of our favourite homes wrapping us in its atoms. As Jabriel's wings hold the entire world, I imagine you, content and warm. I imagine your face. 29—you should have barely aged. I study my own: I was 23, and now I am 27. There is not a significant difference in my appearance. I do not imagine you are tired, ill or haggard; nor devastated, bereft and angered. You are a cat in the sun, body endless, spine and vertebrae pulling so outwards, so forward, a rush of length and growth and suddenly you span the horizon of the world. Have you outgrown me? I am scared I am making a fiction of your memory, of your deserted future. Who am I to entomb time to my desires? Who am I to make you? I wonder of how you have changed, skyward. They say the dead are no longer concerned with material. What happens, then, to your favourite human things? They say your dreams are realised in Barzakh. What do you wish for now, Yousef? Is it selfish to have wanted you to live somehow, miraculously? Yousef, I know your death was a mercy. I wonder if you have seen my grave before I have. Every day, I live through the day I will die. Who will mourn me? I admit I am terrified of it all. You know my fear of the grave. It is all-consuming, haunting. I see you, and I am scared to remember our lives. I mourn you. You knew me our entire lives, and now you are gone. Where do I fit in your new world order? I am no longer a sister alive, attached to you. You cannot embarrass me or tease me or take care of me any longer. We must wait now, however long it takes.

Yousef, I am on a plane and in front of me is a baby who looks like you once looked. Baby fat, cherub cheeks, big smile, windswept curls. I am playing peekaboo with him, wriggling his toes and bumping noses. He is not my baby, but Arabs are always communal. On this flight, another man and I are playing babysitter for two sets of parents. One girl, one boy. I am awash in their laughter. A spy sits next to me. The lasagna was horrible and the plane late. I have spent all day traveling, from Berlin to Frankfurt to Amman. My next moment of joy will be taking off my socks. Do you know I've seen bombs from the sky twice? At first I thought it was thunder. I remember being confused about how there was a storm right then, eating the sky. The bombs flash, cleaving God's sky open. I am in awe of this baby, crying, thinking of you, and to my left are bombs raining. Another massacre. Instead of a killed Palestinian, I saw a dead soldier this afternoon. The taxi driver was from the camps in Lebanon. This baby, Yousef, has his entire life open. Maybe. Maybe not. I regret now the probability that I will not be able to breastfeed my own children. I hope I have my own children before I die. Last week I read about the importance of skin to skin with your child; they fuss less when pulled into your warmth. All I see is you, letting me throw the water on you in Riyadh, both of us too young to use language but still your heart wretched wide open for your baby sister. I love you. Tears so close to you, but never close enough. Yousef, I hope my grave will be easy so I can hold you again. Glory to you, our eternal martyr, my beautiful brother.

ENTRYWAY TO CAPITAL IX
[EMPIRE]

A desire to untoward, a desire of fulfilment, a desire of legacy, a desire of fullness. I pray for your dead as much as I pray for mine. Look! Is not that love? We are all mayflies maybe but what an eternity it is to be alive. You get one chance in this world. Wait for the next. Do you remember before? How softly you were sung into body. Unconditionally you sat in the truth, thick and warm in the breeze. God, I pray to You when every flight takes off. I look at the trees, rotting plumes in the winter, and think how one day I will be them. Tonight, an hour, eighty years. I tell Domingo I am finally an adult when I think of death as happening out of my control. My suicide implied autonomy, agency. The world is terrible, so I will liberate myself. Now, I am 27 and grateful to be in the horrors somehow. Grateful for my lungs, despite their weakness and my bad habits. Death from You is the first agreement we make, fresh and bloody and wet from our mothers' womb. When I die, it is not my will but Yours. Can I be honest? I am scared to die now. There is so much I want to do, so much I live for now, so much brightness I wish the pull in my navel and ribs and hands could do more than mundane magic. I wish I could lick and reconfigure the world entirely. Am I still obedient? My brother dies and I say, *mercy. Unconditional love. I am not scared.* I spent two years crying. On my other brother's 30th birthday, we are stranded on an eleven hour flight back to Amman. My goal is flesh. My meaning is release. Last night I dreamt I was Posideon's daughter, the waves carrying me up to the sky as I waged my wrath on humans. I tell my friends about the dream and Summer says, we have a right to the Greek pantheon and I think yes—yes. Who is Zeus if not Baal? Poseidon if not Yam? Hades if not Mot? The Labours of Hercules mirroring the stories of the Tyrian Melqart. Aphrodite as Ashtar. Adonis as Tammuz. I joke, *I've developed scoliosis from how our ancestors created civilisation time and again.* Here's the punchline: if I was divine, I don't think I would be merciful.

Portal: Cyclical

The genesis of this story is. A person on fire. My father drives us to my brother's grave and I begin to cry seeing a mole trying to cross the heavied street, flush with human monstrosity. Bloomberg announces *empire war supply and demand 1% increase chips SpaceX government approach dig tunnels over a century potential military tool big line of business.* On the way to the graveyard, I tell my father we have no right. This state was a mistake. Last year a raccoon grabbed my finger and we crossed the street together. A white man yells my life is worth more than it and all I think is this is the genesis of empire. The house next to the gates of my loved ones is filled with vultures, domesticated and eerie. My father says, *cycle of nature.* I have been obsessive about my own death the last year, ever since I surpassed my brother. Every rickle of autumn leaves I imagined my decay, the fear of my coming grave haunting me. October, a contour of horrors. I imagine the echoes, but mostly I see children and know they could be mine. I look at my blood and remember empire deems it worthless. The loves of my worlds are meaningless to bombs, despite them being the entirety of my life. I have dreams of my daughters, not yet ready for the world. Every video I look into these childrens' eyes and want, too, for the world to see the fire. A noble martyrdom. When is it enough? Workers of the world. I am so tired of dreaming. I am so scared of movement. I want nothing more than to dissolve the passport in the sea and go home. I would rather die with my children in my arms than live behind this blood.

NEW WORLD ORDER AT THE CENTRE OF MY LOVE

I see your name and watch my heart splinter. Persephone returns and I am done digging a grave. Where have I been buried before? Erect a home of worship atop my name; let me collect and pay off my debts. Sometimes I think I borrowed too much off God; girl made of rizq and luck. I have architected a city out of my love. Come, look, let me show you around! Over here is the fountain (go swimming if you like!), next to it is the library, the seventeen branches of it; the littering smash of cafes and the like; the churches and masajid; the forest and its lake and mountains. The river runs nearby and every summer we all gather at the corniche and its seabed. Everyone in the city has a home. I made it fresh out of love, every single one—yes, of course, I reinforced the beams and stones—I'm not silly, you know, my great-grandfather was an architect back in our city—the other a poet—the other a nuclear physicist. Don't be fooled. I'll never speak, please, when you learn how to read silence and the freckles of my eyes then I will yowl my desires and heart outside, gushing, filling up the fountains. Once a year, I slice my palm open and refill the city; the lights go on and off for a moment then the electricity whizzes right back on. Look, here's the cinema, the pottery classes, the writer's guild, the film studio, the MEMORY MINISTRY—we don't believe in museums here but we did need something a bit official, enforcing some blank we're still not exactly sure how to say. There's the hospital—of course it's so big! Don't be surprised, doesn't everyone deserve to live? Here's the wadi, the farms, and the grooves of the animals and no, it'll be impossible to count their homes. We don't have zoos here, more like Pokémon Centres when they're sick. Look, over here we built the world with them. Ever heard of Noah's Ark? It was like that, but in the urban design meetings. Look, what I'm saying is I have created a world of love for us all.

[*UNDERWORLD*]—THE GIRL, RIVER STYX, A PROMISE, A VOW, FULFILLING!

الخلاص
[SEA]

WHEN WILL YOU LEARN DEATH IS THE ONLY ABSOLUTE? Do not be afraid. My soul spends every night in another realm, a reality more true than what we have bastardised. I love being alive. Do not forget your heart in the garden. Yes, I ate the seeds. Yes, I was dug from the fault-lines and sea-foam. Yes, the portal of my mother's body ached in the gongs of time. My ears rang and rang until I gave birth. Ultra-lush. There is a lust that has reconfigured me, leaving me panting on the street. Can you see it? I am in Rome, lost and aching. I think of you. Can you feel me, still? The light waking us slowly as you found your way around me. Do you mourn your children while they are alive? I mourn everyone I love when I am with them. Life is so quick. An eternity, and yet. I stare at the sea every morning. The seabeds of our childhood, of you, of my love, of my body, of the cool showers in Amman's heatwave and Cairo's dust. I tell my friends we need a Mediterranean Union. I learn Greek at the diner. Etel's ghost summons me. I stare at the painting of Sappho, her hands reaching beyond the cliff's gaze into the rush of the waves. I know the life I want. I am waiting for my hands. I am waiting for you. You said you are not scared of death when I cried. I never told you I cried for you.

Friday, Amman (16 August)

The prophecy: my heart is open and I am a sea, a movement of love and its eternity. The sea of love to be split, spilling, drenched, consuming. How beautiful the waves fall, the tide of love in its movement. Habibi. I cannot tell you my favourite moments of the film in our love. Only that an eternity hummed its light, pulsing slowly between our hands. I returned home early and spent the day in the ecstasy of yearning; the breath of our futures pulling together like a new-born tree. The ease in which we love. The realms are swaying in my acceptance. I am so sorry I ran late, habibi. Can I have another kiss?

[*THE SEA*]—THE GIRL, HER SWORD, WAVES CRASHING TO MEET HER, HER GHOSTS RESTING ALONGSIDE HER. THE LIVING, STILL, STILL!!!

Persephone's Sword

Dance with me, your hand on my hip. Listen for the beggars. Call for mercy. Do you have a shekel to spare? I lost my gold in Amman and wept for months. Where have you touched me? I closed my eyes and the sky fell. Glory. Transparency. Lie of a small oppression. Photograph of grief: my father curled towards the window, bereft of his son. يا ضناي. I would give the world to you. In Frankfurt Airport, I bought a 30 minute shower and cried the entire way through. There is always a before and after. I no longer remember who I was before your death. I collect photographs to remember what I looked like once. I am amazed every time that I find myself beautiful in the midst of it all. July. October. Have you grieved enough? Sometimes I imagine Cairo now, how different it is with no one left for me to love inside it. Are we drawing up new names for the seas and its prophecies? There's a river gleaming, golden mists, glided stones crushed on the tongue of waves. To be human is to despair, wretched in devastation. To be human is to ride a train to Alex, collapse on the seabed and find eternity in our love. Look, the world has ended. Do you see it too? That doesn't mean there isn't something still worth living for. The grotesque horrifies me, others find solace in it. Why make lust from a feverish human lost in limbo between species? Love will reinvent you. I am made from all the people who love me. I know exactly who I am. Why do you still believe we are made out of images and not hearts? Are we all martyrs? My brother will take seven. Only God can dissolve me. Only God can judge me. Go back. There is still time. Why are you so ready to transcend humanity? There are no flowers on the moon. You know I love the sea. I love being human. I love this earth. I love my grief. I love my desire. I am not meant for this. I am not meant to flee from the horrors of my humanity. The wind is calling. Persephone, our language a secret. Our bodies, held sweet. I'll see you soon. The afterlife is home as much as the sea and the land. My sword, my gentle sword. You are a part of me still.

Eulogy
28 June, 1995 - 2 July, 2020

Yousef Aboutaleb is a beloved son, brother, and friend. His hopes encased a vision for a world overflowing in love. His heart, too kind and big, was a treasure vault of mercy and tenderness. His smile was as bright as the sun, crammed with perfect teeth solely because they belonged to him and showed our inheritance from our brilliant parents. Yousef brought his love and care into making a kinder world in everything he did. His love for history, the land, and the seas mobilised him into community and action in ways I wish I could articulate.

I cannot speak for anyone else who grieves my brother. In losing him, the world has lost a man so white-hearted that it felt heaven was embodied within him.

Yousef, since your death time has become eternal. I see you everywhere, in the shade of the trees and the warmth of the sun. Every June, I return to the midst of grief, heavy and catastrophic.

Nothing I say will ever give you a shadow of my brother. I can regale you all with a thousand memories, and still the sharpness of loss will not be so fulfilled. The world has lost a man who it never deserved.

My brother was one of the kindest people I have ever had the honour of knowing and loving. In his memory, I have strove to open my heart and be sincere in my love. In him, I will always carry our childhood selves. We are still alive somewhere together, still a brother and sister and brother entangled on the corniche shouting in the wind, throwing ourselves headfirst into the sea. There is nothing more I will ever want than to be running in time with him again.

إنا لله و إنا إليه راجعون

Notes

Earlier versions of some poems appear, some in different forms or under different names, in the following publications:

"elegy (i): the grave" in *ANMLY.*

"Ramadan" and "Languaging Memory" in *Poetry Online.*

"Hijacked Interiors" in *Strange Horizons* with thanks to Vanessa Jae for her solicitation.

"Spectral Memory" and "Mythos" in *Poetry Ireland Review*, with thanks to Theo Dorgan for his curation.

"October" in *Mizna.*

"Inheritance" in *Prairie Schooner*, with thanks to Lena Khalaf Tuffaha for her curation.

"What about witnessing do you want to remember?" in *The Columbia Journal*, with thanks to Mariam Syed for her curation.

"Portal: Cyclical" in *Split This Rock*, with thanks to Gowri Konsewaran for her curation.

This work was supported by the McCormack Writing Center (formerly the Tin House Workshop) in its Summer 2024 Workshop, as well as Kundiman in its 2024 Summer Retreat.

Poems after Sappho are worked from *If Not, Winter*, pages 61-95.

Etel, the Oracle, is after Etel Adnan.

"Wind Waker" is after Summer Farah.

"elegy (i): the grave" is after and has lines from Diana Khoi Nguyen's "*Ghost Of.*"

"Memory, Isle of Blest" is after and has lines from JinJin Xu's "*There Is Still Singing in The Afterlife*."

"This Horrifying Earth" is after and has lines from JinJin Xu's "*Against This Earth, We Knock*"

"Graveyard Visits" is after and has lines from JinJin Xu's "*To Red Dust (II)*."

Acknowledgements

A special thank you to my mother, my father, and my brothers. I could write essays on how grateful I am to be yours, but for now, know I only know how to love from you. For my dead and my living, I thank you for everything. I love you all.

Mama, you gave me a home and a briefcase. You gave me your soul and taught me the shape of my own. In the quiet moment of my devastation, I left my city and met your exile as a landing pad. Baba, the river and the seas you gave us; the mango trees and laughter; the sprawling city that has held my love, my heart, my eyes. For the blood you both shed to give us life.

For my brothers, no matter what, there is nothing I would not do for you both.

For Palestine, always and forever. For my family and the homes you built in us. For Palestinians everywhere, in this life and the next. There are no words in this language to hold your honour. For all the oppressed people in this world, may justice and liberation be yours. May we burn a new world order together.

Thank you to Julia, Domingo, Jessi and Summer. To Newfie and Suha for keeping me afloat. To Youssef, my film partner. To my beautiful community for your unending support, love, and care: Alex, Fargo, Aiya, Sima, Faris, Dalia, Lara, Noor, George, Ruanne, Mayss, Hamzah, Hana, Emad and to many, many others.

Thank you to my friends in Cairo and Amman, and to those who listen and continue building a life with me. Thank you to those holding a piece of my heart and taking care of it, across all our cities, waters, and languages.

Thank you to Tracy Fuad, who during class at the Berlin Writers Workshop, told me, at a gentle 32 pages into this project, that I was writing my debut.

To our beautiful workshop crew from Tin House who taught me how to read with a generous rigour amongst many other questions of direction, stakes, and heat. To everything our cohort has locked and linked in together.

Thank you to the publications who took in my pieces, the supportive editors, and the literary community, especially at Mizna and RAWI, in caring for our communities.

Thank you to the dream team at Game Over Books, who believed so much in *THALASSA*—from Josh (bestie) to Giovanna (world's best publicist!).

Thank you to Summer Farah for editing this manuscript with her generosity and rigour; for her decade long friendship and the worlds we inhabit together.

Thank you to Grace Pastore for working with me to design this cover, the visual monument of this five-year long project, crafted in her incredible and patient hands.

Thank you to my wonderful blurbers: Fargo Nissim Tbakhi, Jessica Rizkallah, JinJin Xu, and Sarah Ghazal Ali for spending time with my poems and holding these words in such kindness and warmth. I cannot express my gratitude and appreciation for seeing myself and *THALASSA* in your eyes.

Thank you to Rumi Cafe for letting me kick it for years, where the majority of this book was written. To all the homies in Amman who passed me falafel sandwiches, coffees on the house, and a supportive community who kept me furnished and alive during the most difficult time of my life. To Amman, for giving me my two little cats, along with the 26 in my garden who always kept me company.

Finally, thank you to the Game Stop associate at the Catonsville H-Mart plaza who told my father in 2004 that *Legend of Zelda: Wind Waker* was the perfect gift for his three children eagerly awaiting his return to Kuwait.

Baba, Mama, thank you for everything. Kareem, you have never let us have the controller unless threatened. Yousef, I love you.

I am grateful for everyone who was with me during the early years of my grief, and for those who will now carry a small part of my beautiful brother and our love for him with you. It is my hope that in this book, you will find your own seabed to rest in.

leena aboutaleb is an Egyptian and Palestinian writer who asks you to commit to the Palestinian liberation struggle. She is the author of THALASSA (Game Over Books, 2026). Her pamphlet, Expeditions of Projection, was released in 2023 (VIBE). Her film, 'Oracle,' co-produced with Youssef ElNahas debuted in Venice, 2025. She is a Brooklyn Poets fellow, a Kundiman fellow and Tin House scholar. Read her work at www.leenaboutaleb.onl.

www.ingramcontent.com/pod-product-compliance
Lightning Source LLC
LaVergne TN
LVHW021200160826
845679LV00024B/2178

* 9 7 9 8 9 9 4 8 1 1 2 7 6 *